The Polish Americans

DONNA LOCK

MAJOR AMERICAN IMMIGRATION

MASON CREST PUBLISHERS • PHILADELPHIA

Youngsters march in the Polish Constitution Day parade on May 6, 2000, in Chicago. The parade celebrates the anniversary of the Poles' first constitution, which was signed on May 3, 1791. It is considered to be the first democratic constitution in Europe.

The Polish Americans

DONNA LOCK

MAJOR AMERICAN IMMIGRATION

MASON CREST PUBLISHERS • PHILADELPHIA

Mason Crest Publishers
370 Reed Road
Broomall PA 19008
www.masoncrest.com

Copyright © 2009 by Mason Crest Publishers. All rights reserved.
Printed and bound in Malaysia.

First printing

1 3 5 7 9 8 6 4 2

Library of Congress Cataloging-in-Publication Data

Lock, Donna.
   The Polish Americans / Donna Lock.
      p. cm. — (Major American immigration)
   Includes index.
   ISBN 978-1-4222-0616-4 (hardcover)
   ISBN 978-1-4222-0683-6 (pbk.)
   1. Polish Americans—Juvenile literature. 2. Polish Americans—
History—Juvenile literature. 3. Immigrants—United States—
History—Juvenile literature. 4. United States—Ethnic relations—
Juvenile literature. I. Title.
   E184.P7M715 2008
   973'.049185—dc22
                                              2008026008

Table of Contents

Introduction: America's Ethnic Heritage
      Barry Moreno 7

1 The Story of Adam Laboda 11

2 Leaving Their Homeland 17

3 Moving to New Locations 23

4 Seeking Jobs and Opportunities 31

5 Building New Lives 41

6 Current Immigration 51

Chronology 54

Immigration Figures 55

Famous Polish Immigrants 56

Glossary 58

Further Reading 60

Internet Resources 61

Index 62

MAJOR AMERICAN IMMIGRATION

THE AFRICAN AMERICANS

THE ARAB AMERICANS

THE CHINESE AMERICANS

CITIZENSHIP: RIGHTS AND RESPONSIBILITIES

THE CUBAN AMERICANS

THE GERMAN AMERICANS

HISTORY OF AMERICAN IMMIGRATION

THE IRISH AMERICANS

THE ITALIAN AMERICANS

THE JAPANESE AMERICANS

THE JEWISH AMERICANS

THE KOREAN AMERICANS

THE MEXICAN AMERICANS

THE NATIVE AMERICANS

THE POLISH AMERICANS

THE RUSSIAN AMERICANS

America's Ethnic Heritage

Barry Moreno, librarian

Statue of Liberty/

Ellis Island National Monument

E thnic diversity is one of the most striking characteristics of the American identity. In the United States the Bureau of the Census officially recognizes 122 different ethnic groups. North America's population had grown by leaps and bounds, starting with the American Indian tribes and nations—the continent's original people—and increasing with the arrival of the European colonial migrants who came to these shores during the 16th and 17th centuries. Since then, millions of immigrants have come to America from every corner of the world.

But the passage of generations and the great distance of America from the "Old World"—Europe, Africa, and Asia—has in some cases separated immigrant peoples from their roots. The struggle to succeed in America made it easy to forget past traditions. Further, the American spirit of freedom, individualism, and equality gave Americans a perspective quite different from the view of life shared by residents of the Old World.

Immigrants of the 19th and 20th centuries recognized this at once. Many tried to "Americanize" themselves by tossing away their peasant clothes and dressing American-style even before reaching their new homes in the cities or the countryside of America. It was not so easy to become part of America's culture, however. For many immigrants, learning English was quite a hurdle. In fact, most older immigrants clung to the old ways, preferring to speak their native languages and follow their familiar customs and traditions. This was easy to do when ethnic neighborhoods abounded in large North American cities like New York, Montreal, Philadelphia, Chicago, Toronto, Boston, Cleveland, St. Louis, New Orleans and San Francisco. In rural areas, farm families—many of them Scandinavian, German, or Czech—established their own tightly knit communities. Thus foreign languages and dialects, religious beliefs, Old World customs, and certain class distinctions flourished.

The most striking changes occurred among the children of immigrants, whose hopes and dreams were different from those of their parents. They began breaking away from the Old World customs, perhaps as a reaction to the embarrassment of being labeled "foreigner." They badly wanted to be Americans, and assimilated more easily than their parents and grandparents. They learned to speak English without a foreign accent, to dress and act like other Americans. The assimilation of the children of immigrants was encouraged by social contact—games, schools, jobs, and military service—which further broke down the barriers between immigrant groups and hastened the process of Americanization. Along the way, many family traditions were lost or abandoned.

Today, the pride that Americans have in their ethnic roots is one of the abiding strengths of both the United States and Canada. It shows that the theory which called America a "melting pot" of the world's people was never really true. The thought that a single "American" would emerge from the combination of these peoples has never happened, for Americans have grown more reluctant than ever before to forget the struggles of their ethnic forefathers. The growth of cultural studies and genealogical research indicates that Americans are anxious not to entirely lose this identity, whether it is English, French, Chinese, African, Mexican, or some other group. There is an interest in tracing back the family line as far as records or memory will take them. In a sense, this has made Americans a divided people; proud to be Americans, but proud also of their ethnic roots.

As a result, many Americans have welcomed a new identity, that of the hyphenated American. This unique description has grown in usage over the years and continues to grow as more Americans recognize the importance of family heritage. In the end, this is an appreciation of America's great cultural heritage and its richness of its variety.

This photograph of an immigrant couple from Poland was taken in the late 19th century. Polish immigrants sometimes faced discrimination when they arrived in the United States.

1 The Story of Adam Laboda

People have been moving to new locations throughout history. Often, the move was from one town to another or between regional areas. However, people have also *emigrated*, or left their native country to move to another country. These moves were sometimes forced on people by governments. In other situations, individuals made the choice to move. Men and women who have moved to a new country are called *immigrants*. Many individuals have left their homes and families to move to America and build a new life. Their voyage was not easy, and the immigrants struggled to find their own place in a new country. This was the case for Adam Laboda, a young male immigrant from Poland.

Adam Laboda was born in Zowisezbie, Poland, in 1875, the oldest son in a family of nine boys and two girls. He and his family lived in a two-room house on a farm. The Labodas raised both crops and animals—cattle, pigs, geese, ducks, and chickens—to provide food for themselves. There was not much time for play for Adam and his siblings because of school and the farm. "We got up at 5 o'clock in the morning and worked 'til dark," Adam later remembered. "We had only kerosene lamps and we worked hard in daylight all the time."

At the age of 12, Adam's father asked him to find a job to help support the family. Adam moved to Germany and worked as a spinner in a mill. After two years, he returned to the farm in Poland.

Adam's uncle had moved to Syracuse, New York, earlier. He wrote to the family about coming to America. A group of 14 boys from Zowisezbie decided to travel to America with an adult man as their leader. "The boys were all from 14 to 16 years of age. This was in the great emigration period from 1890 to 1902," recalled Adam. "We took a train and traveled two days to Bremen [a city in Germany]. There we took ship and voyaged for 12 days. We landed in New York Harbor and then went up the river to Albany on another boat and took a train to Gilbertsville, Massachusetts, where there are big woolen mills. I had a friend there and I got a job in the spinning room."

Adam and his friends rented rooms from Polish people who lived in houses owned by the company. There were four boys in a room, and each paid $3 per month. "There were about 24 of us in one house. We bought our own groceries and gave them to the woman who kept the house, and she cooked for us. We earned $2.77 a week and worked 64 hours a week, then we got up to $4.76 a week. It cost only four cents a loaf for bread and four cents a pound for meat but we had no chance to go to shows or anything," said Adam. "After nine years, I was earning $8.12 a week and I had got ahead faster than some of the older men, who got only $5.08 a week."

There were also many Polish girls working in the mill, and a favorite activity for the Polish immigrants was dancing. "Our best fun was dancing in the [dancing] houses, and then the company built a dance hall for us so that it cost nothing to dance," said Adam.

Anna and John Tifs of Adams, Massachusetts, wrote the following letter to Mary Ekelman of Lawki, Poland, in December 1890:

Dear Sister!

I received your letter and I will satisfy your request. I am sending a steamship ticket for you and the child and 25 rubles [a small sum of money] for the trip. Sell whatever you have at home, potatoes or other things. When you arrive in New York where they will be entering your names into a book, show them the envelope which I am enclosing in this letter, and tell them that the one whose address is on it is going to buy a ticket for the trip here [Adams, Massachusetts]. Keep that envelope with you and the card, which is in the envelope giving my address, show it to them, then they [the customs people] will know where you are to go....Take a winter shawl, good warm clothes for the child so that he will be warm, and a pillow for him....Try not to make any mistakes, go direct....If God will bring you safely across, it will be better for you here. Keep well.

In 1908, Adam returned to Poland to visit his family. He married a Polish girl who had also worked in Gilbertsville while he was there. The two of them returned to America. "When I wanted to get married, I did not want to rent but to have a tenement of my own, and the company houses could not be bought here," said Adam. "I came to Pittsfield [Massachusetts] where they told me I could get a job

An accordion player waves as she marches in a parade. When emigrants from Poland arrived in the United States and Canada, they often moved to communities where other Polish immigrants lived. The close-knit fabric of life in these communities helped Polish Americans keep certain elements of Polish culture.

with Berkshire Woolen, but when I got here, they told me to
go to Pontoosuc as I would get a better job. Well, I could not talk
English yet and I worked there one day and then the boss told me
I would have to go. I did not know why. He paid me $1.50, and I
went back to Berkshire Woolen. The boss at Pontoosuc was Irish.
He is dead now. I was a Polack. You see, I did not know why I
was fired at first."

After Adam returned to work at the Berkshire Woolen Mill, he
became an expert spinner. He worked at the mill for more than 30
years. He and his wife had five children, some of whom also worked at
the Berkshire factory. Eventually, Adam became a **naturalized** citizen
of the United States.

The settlement at Jamestown, founded in 1608, was the first permanent English settlement in North America. Among the settlers were several craftsmen from the region that today is Poland.

2 Leaving Their Homeland

The first record of Polish immigration to America dates to 1608 in Jamestown, Virginia. The Poles were skilled glassblowers and woodworkers and were **recruited** by the colonists for their talents. The immigrants were also hard workers and were knowledgeable about building materials. The Poles built a furnace and began creating glass. Their glass products were sold to Europe and were among the first American-made products **exported** to other countries. They helped to establish the early glassmaking and woodworking industries in the colonies.

The next wave of immigration occurred between 1800 and 1860. Records from the U.S. Immigration and Naturalization Service indicate that fewer than 2,000 Polish citizens entered the United States during that time. Most of these people left Poland for political reasons.

In 1854, 800 Polish Catholics founded Panna Maria, a farming community in east Texas. This community established the first Polish-Catholic church and school in the United States.

Soon, the mass migration from Poland to the United States began. Between 1860 and 1910, 2.5 million Poles arrived in North America. This period is often referred to as the "Great Migration." The Poles were the third-largest immigrant group arriving in the

United States during the late 19th century and the early 20th century. Some Poles immigrated to Canada as well.

The end of the 19th century brought many changes to Poland, and Polish citizens were unhappy about these changes. The country lost its independence because of expansion by its neighbors, Russia, Prussia, and Austria. Most of the immigrants were **peasant** farmers who wanted to improve their life. High birthrates, large populations, and changing agricultural conditions made farming a difficult situation in Poland. The Polish farmers had been living in poverty and were anxious to work in the United States where wages were much higher.

Religious freedom and forced military service were two other factors that convinced people to leave Poland. Other immigrants decided to leave based on advertisements from employers seeking help. Encouraging letters sent home by new arrivals in the United States also prompted individuals to leave. The letters were passed around in the villages or published in newspapers. Steel mill owners and meatpacking and mining foremen often encouraged immigrant employees to write home asking for other Poles to come to the United States and work for their companies.

It was common for one member of a family to go to America first, then save money to bring more relatives over. The immigrants who had arrived earlier would send prepaid tickets to Poland for the next family member. It is estimated that in 1890 between 25 and 50 percent of all immigrants arriving in America had prepaid tickets.

A potter in Jamestown crafts a vessel on his wheel. Polish settlers in the English colony also made glass objects and worked with wood.

Thaddeus Kosciuszko (1746–1817) was a Polish officer who had a distinguished career with the Continental Army during the Revolutionary War. As a young man, Kosciuszko spent three years as a student and instructor at the Royal School for Cadets in Warsaw. He was promoted to captain. Following five years of studies in France, he decided to sail to America after hearing reports about the start of the American Revolution.

Kosciuszko approached the Continental Congress in Philadelphia in 1776 and was appointed colonel of engineers. His engineering work at West Point was key to an American victory there. He also led American troops into Charleston, South Carolina. By the end of the war in 1783, he had been promoted to brigadier general.

Kosciuszko returned to Poland in 1784, where he led a revolt against Russia. After his capture, he was asked not to return to Poland. He moved back to Philadelphia and renewed his friendship with Thomas Jefferson. When he left America again, he asked Jefferson to be the *executor* of his estate and asked that his money be used to buy and free slaves. Kosciuszko died in 1817 in Switzerland.

In 1925, on the 150th anniversary of Kosciuszko's enlistment in the Continental Army, the Kosciuszko Foundation was established. The foundation was designed to promote education and cultural exchanges between the United States and Poland.

In 1901, between 40 and 65 percent of all immigrants traveled on prepaid tickets or with money sent to them.

Many of the immigrants who left Poland were young men. There were several reasons why so many young men chose to emigrate. For one thing, jobs were easier to find in North America than in Poland. Many of the young men planned to only stay a few years and work hard, then return to Poland as wealthy citizens. Just as Adam Laboda did, many Polish immigrants traveled with a group to a town where they had a contact person. This contact person was able to help the young men in obtaining jobs and homes. They also taught the newcomers about their new country. ✴

Emigrants from Poland and Czechoslovakia board a ship in Southampton, England, that will take them to America. For much of the 19th century Russia controlled Poland, and in 1863 the country was blended into Russia. This led many Poles to decide to leave their home country and move to America.

3 Moving to New Locations

Like most immigrants at this time, traveling to North America for Polish immigrants involved an ocean journey. Prior to the 1870s, people would travel in cramped quarters located in the bottom of a sailing ship. The voyage would take about two months. Steamships then began to replace sailing ships, which lowered ticket prices and reduced travel time to two weeks.

Many tickets were sold for the *steerage* compartment—the lowest deck of the ship—because there were no rooms or space requirements. The shipping lines often sold more tickets to travelers than they could accommodate. Steamships normally carried about 1,000 passengers, but occasionally over 1,500 people were packed onto a ship. The shipping companies promoted their voyages by hiring agents to sell tickets and tell prospective immigrants about the advantages of moving to North America. The agents traveled from village to village in Europe spreading the word about the opportunities available.

It was not easy for the immigrants to get to the port from which the ship would sail. They often traveled by train, wagon, donkey, horse, or on foot to get to the port. The immigrants often had to wait several days or a month for the ship to arrive before they could sail to North America. In some ports, the steamship companies had *dormitories* for the immigrants to stay in and provided them with food until their ship arrived.

Passengers continued to travel in cramped, dirty quarters on the steamships. Smoked, dried, or salted foods were served to the travelers in addition to any food that they had brought aboard the ship. Due to the unhealthy accommodations, many passengers became sick with cholera, typhus, and other diseases. Seasickness was also a problem for people.

Space was limited on the ship, so the passengers could only bring items that they could carry. Some immigrants had trunks or suitcases, but many only carried bundles tied with string. It was not uncommon to see people wearing several layers of clothing to save room for other items. Pillows and bedding were among the items that the immigrants brought on the voyage. They slept on narrow bunk beds, and the temperature was cold in the lower decks. Many of the Poles sold or gave away most of their possessions before traveling to North America. The immigrants would visit the top deck as often as possible. It was common to see the passengers dancing and playing music. Many of the Poles would practice speaking English and talk about their dreams for America.

About 75 percent of all immigrants entering the United States during the great wave of migration went through the Ellis Island immigration station in New York. Prior to 1892, many immigrants entered the United States through Castle Garden on Manhattan. As the steamships entered the harbor, the first thing most people saw was the Statue of Liberty. This statue symbolized hope and dreams of the future for the newcomers. A Polish man said, "The bigness of Ms. Liberty overcame us. No one spoke a word, for she was like a goddess and we knew she represented the big, powerful country which was to be our future home."

After arriving in New York, the passengers were taken by ferry to Ellis Island for inspections. The newcomers were given tags with numbers on them to wear that indicated the page and line of the ship's *manifest* on which their name appeared.

The immigrants stood in long lines and walked single file to their medical examinations in the Registry Room. This large room contained a maze of aisles. Doctors would examine each person's face, hair, neck, and hands. He would place a chalk mark on their

This drawing from an 1881 issue of *Harper's Weekly,* a popular magazine of the late 19th century, shows health officials vaccinating Polish and Russian immigrants on board the steamship *Victoria.* One woman is being restrained, and men are fighting in the background.

clothing if any problems were detected. Approximately 2 out of every 10 immigrants would receive a large white letter. These individuals were separated from their families or traveling companions and sent to dormitories where they received medical care. They were often bathed with a disinfectant to remove germs.

A family from Poland arrives at Ellis Island in December 1949, holding out their landing cards to a smiling guard. The Swobodas and their 10 children arrived aboard the ship *General Muir.* They were headed to Shelby, North Carolina, to work on a farm.

Many immigrants were reunited with their families after treatment, but some were **deported** if their health did not improve in a few days. Sick children over the age of 12 were sent back to the port that they had sailed from. Children younger than 12 were sent back with a parent. A Polish immigrant named Regina Sass Tepper recalled, "When you went to sleep you were afraid that maybe somebody was going to come during the night and pull you out and say, 'Well, you're sick. Come on, we'll send you back'. You lived in constant fear of being sent back."

A legal inspection was conducted following the medical examination. The inspectors were often from immigrant families and spoke several different languages. Questions regarding age, place of birth, name, occupation, and destination were asked. This inspection took only a few minutes due to the large number of people coming through Ellis Island. It was at this point that many names of the immigrants were changed or spelled incorrectly. Many of the inspectors did not understand the names or did not take the time to write the name correctly.

Many immigrants showed letters from friends and relatives in the United States to the inspectors. Single women were allowed to enter only if

Reporters from *The Independent,* a newspaper in New York City at the beginning of the 20th century, interviewed many immigrants who entered the United States at Ellis Island. Their stories were printed in the newspaper. The following excerpt is from a Jewish immigrant from Poland: "We came by steerage on a steamship in a very dark place that smelt dreadfully. There were hundreds of other people packed in with us, men, women, and children, and almost all of them were sick. It took us 12 days to cross the sea, and we thought we should die, but at last the voyage was over, and we came up and saw the beautiful bay and the big woman with the spikes on her head and the lamp that is lighted at night in her hand [the Statue of Liberty]."

Many of the Polish immigrants to the United States came through Ellis Island, the processing station in New York harbor. Between 1892 and 1954, more than 12 million immigrants passed through Ellis Island. Today, approximately 100 million Americans can claim ancestry to someone who arrived in America at Ellis Island.

they had a sponsor and a written document, such as a letter or telegraph message, from the sponsor. Unaccompanied single women and children were held at Ellis Island until a relative came to meet them.

The railroad ticket office at Ellis Island was the next stop for those newcomers traveling to destinations outside of New York City. During busy times, as many as 25 tickets per minute would be sold to immigrants.

The final step for the newcomers was to ride the ferry from Ellis Island to Manhattan. Some of the immigrants would stay in New York City while others headed to various destinations, often by railroad or boat. Sponsors, contact persons, and other family members would arrange to meet the immigrants at these places.

Ellis Island remained a port of entry for immigrants entering the United States until it was closed in 1954. Through preservation efforts, the port was restored and the Ellis Island Immigration Museum opened in 1990. The museum honors the history of immigration and the role of Ellis Island. Visitors can view the Registry Room, dormitory room, railroad ticket office, and other exhibits. The American Immigrant Wall of Honor has more than 500,000 names listed on it as a memorial to immigrants.

Polish immigrants also arrived in Canada, but in much smaller numbers. In the late 19th century Canada did not have an official immigrant port of entry such as Ellis Island. Officials inspected boats when they arrived in Quebec City, Vancouver, or Montreal. Canada had few restrictions on the incoming arrivals and eagerly welcomed newcomers to their country. ✷

A man works steel in a mill in Pittsburgh, Pennsylvania. Many of the millions of Polish immigrants who arrived in the late 19th century settled near large cities and worked in steel mills, coal mines, meatpacking plants, and other industries.

4 Seeking Jobs and Opportunities

Many of the earliest Polish immigrants settled in farming states in the United States: the Panna Maria community in Texas, Wisconsin, Minnesota, South Dakota, and North Dakota. Beginning in the 1880s, Poles began to settle in industrial cities where unskilled laborers were needed. Most of these immigrants arrived in the United States after the big westward expansion and moved to cities in the northeast. By 1900, 95 percent were working in coal mining, steel, meatpacking, textile mills, automobile factories, and other industries.

New immigrants followed other friends and family members to specific areas instead of traveling to unknown communities. Cities such as Chicago, Detroit, Pittsburgh, Cleveland, Milwaukee, and Buffalo had large Polish populations. Polish immigrants who were already working as laborers helped the newcomers find jobs and housing. Most of the Poles were peasants with little education and skills, but they adapted easily to the factory jobs.

The Polish immigrant population was estimated at 50,000 in Pittsburgh in 1903. The immigrant's life was difficult with low wages and long days. Most of the Poles were employed in steel mills, where the average steelworker received $1.50 per day and worked 72 hours a week. Many worked in the open *hearths*, which involved long hours and had a high risk of injury. Lighting and ventilation were poor, and there were few safety measures. Shifts were usually 12 hours, but sometimes the steel workers were forced to work the dangerous 24-hour "long turn" shift, where accidents were common.

Polish immigrants also settled in western Pennsylvania, where jobs in the coal mines were plentiful. The miners lived in areas called "patch villages" that were owned by the mining companies. Houses, company stores, schools, and churches were part of the patch village and also owned by the coal company. Each immigrant group clustered together in their own section of the village. The company store sold items, such as flour, sugar, fabric, and mining supplies, at high prices. However, the miners were forced to buy items they needed from the company store. Purchases were deducted from the paycheck of the miners. Often, the immigrants' pay did not cover their purchases, and they would owe money to the company store.

The immigrants worked 12 or more hours a day, six days a week. The miners worked underground in narrow passageways on their hands and knees. They worked in poor conditions for low wages. Some miners were killed due to unsafe practices.

Many of the immigrants banded together to complain about the low pay and poor working conditions. They wanted the coal companies to provide better housing and do away with the company store. The miners held several small *strikes* to draw the attention of mine owners to their complaints. However, conditions did not improve for the miners.

On September 10, 1897, a group of 400 striking immigrant coal miners marched to Pardee Mine in Lattimer, Pennsylvania. The majority

A boy stokes a coal-burning stove near the center of this picture of eastern European immigrants working in a metal shop in the United States. Polish immigrants often worked long hours for low wages in Pittsburgh and other industrial cities.

Many Polish children were anxious to be like other Americans and tried to hide their heritage from other groups. Some Poles adopted nicknames and changed their dress in an effort to find their place in America. In the book *Ellis Island: An Illustrated History of the Immigrant Experience,* Louise Nagy talks about how she wanted to be known as an American, not a Polish immigrant, in 1913. "We wanted to be Americans so quickly that we were embarrassed if our parents couldn't speak English. My father was reading a Polish paper, and somebody was supposed to come to the house. I remember sticking it under something. We were that ashamed of being foreign."

of these miners were Poles. The striking miners were unarmed and carried a large American flag. A sheriff and 60 deputies hid behind cover and shot at 40 of the immigrants. Of the 19 striking miners that were killed, 14 were Polish immigrants. Numerous others were wounded. This event, known as the Lattimer Massacre, marked the beginning of the labor movement in the coal industry. As word of this tragedy spread to other Polish immigrants, they became more convinced that an organized effort was needed to change things in the United States. As a result, the Poles became strong supporters of organized labor unions in America.

About one-third of the Poles continued their farming practices
in the United States. They established farms on abandoned land
in Long Island, grew tobacco and onions in the Connecticut Valley
of western Massachusetts, and planted corn and wheat in Wisconsin
and Minnesota.

Unlike in Poland, Polish women and girls had jobs outside of the home.
Immigrant families were poor and needed the wages of every available
family member. They worked as seamstresses, household servants, tailors,
or factory workers. Polish women also opened their homes to boarders
such as Adam Laboda. This work was hard, because the women were
responsible for cooking, cleaning, and doing laundry for as many as 12
men in addition to their own families. Other women operated saloons
in their homes where the Poles would gather to drink and socialize.

Work in the coal mines
of Pennsylvania was
dirty, as this picture
of a miner shows. It
also was very dangerous.
Bad treatment by mine
owners led Poles to form
the earliest labor unions
in the United States.

During the early 20th century, quota laws were passed to slow the flood of emigrants from eastern Europe. This political cartoon shows Uncle Sam limiting the annual immigration to 3 percent of the total population already living in the country.

Among the earliest Polish immigrants to arrive in Canada was a group from northern Poland called Kashubs. Canada was actively recruiting people to move and offered free land to settlers who would move there. Shipping agents traveled to areas of Poland in which the residents were poor and in desperate situations to promote these opportunities. The agents made the free land offer and sent the Poles to Canada on sailing ships. The first group of 76 people arrived in 1858. Additional groups of Kashubs followed in later years.

Polish immigrants arriving in Canada settled in urban communities close to Toronto, Montreal, and Ontario. More than 115,000 Polish settlers came to Canada between 1896 and 1918. The immigrants honored their homeland by naming one area in northern Ontario "Kaszuby." Many of these people helped build the Canadian Pacific Railway or worked in copper and nickel mines. The Poles also received land grants for **homesteading** or purchased farms in Ontario, Manitoba, Alberta, and Saskatchewan.

The Poles, along with other immigrants, faced **discrimination** in North America. Not everyone was happy with the large numbers of immigrants arriving in the United States. Longtime Americans did not welcome the newcomers into their county. Many Americans resented the Poles for settling in their neighborhoods because of their different language, customs, and dress. Forgetting that they had also once traveled to America from another country and had suffered prejudices, they displayed negative attitudes toward the Poles. Furthermore, many of the earlier immigrants from western Europe argued that the new immigrants, mainly from Eastern Europe, were inferior and had low intelligence. In the early 1900s, studies by nongovernmental agencies depicted the Poles as **illiterate** and criminals.

The Poles also suffered discrimination in the workplace. Managers preferred to hire Americans first for skilled positions, followed by Irish, Scots, English, Welsh, Germans, and then Poles. This practice prevented Poles from working in higher-level jobs that paid more and kept them in the lower-paying jobs, which were less safe. Immigrants such as Adam Laboda were fired or not offered a job because they were from Poland. Many Americans called them "Polacks" or foreigners.

This letter was written from Maks Markiewicz to his cousin Waclaw Markiewicz on October 5, 1909. Maks had immigrated to the United States seven years earlier, and Waclaw was a recent immigrant from Poland. The term "brother" is often used for male relatives:

Dear Brother Waclaw:

I inform you about an offer from which you will perhaps profit. My old boss told me today that he had much work, so perhaps I knew some carpenters, and if so, I should send them to him. I told him that I had a brother carpenter who was working, but if the work would be steady, I could bring him. He answered that he hoped to have steady work. So I advise you to come, dear brother....we could live here in the foreign land together....We could meet him in South Chicago and speak about the business.

Maks

The Polish immigrants were often fearful about these prejudices. Some Poles changed their names to sound more American so that they would not be singled out. Other immigrants began to use American nicknames or spell their names differently. "At school I went as Thomas," one man recalled, "because my teacher would not pronounce or spell my own [name]." A child of Polish-American parents remembered that she never raised her hand in elementary school to speak. "I was afraid I'd make a mistake...American children called us 'Hunky'....We felt inferior."

Laborers were not happy that businesses were hiring the immigrants to avoid strikes and to keep wages low. Many labor leaders favored limiting the number of immigrants into America to protect the workers that were already here.

The United States Congress decided to reduce the number of immigrants from Eastern Europe that would be allowed to enter the country. This reduction had a direct effect on immigrants from Poland. Congress passed new immigration laws during the 1920s. These laws established **quotas** for each country using a formula that favored immigrants from western European countries, such as England and Germany.

The Polish immigrants who came to Canada also experienced similar cases of discrimination and prejudice. Name-calling and fights were common occurrences for Poles. In Kaszuby, Poles lived among immigrants of Irish descent, and there was frequent hostility between the two groups. ✺

This aerial view shows the Polish neighborhood
of Hamtramck in Detroit, Michigan. As is common
with Polish-American communities, a large
Roman Catholic church has been built at the
center of the neighborhood.

5 Building New Lives

The majority of people who lived in Poland were Roman Catholic. Their life was centered on the church, the community, and the family. As the Poles immigrated to North America, they carried their strong religious beliefs along with them to their new country. The immigrants first met in groups at stores or hotels. As the group expanded, parishes were formed by priests who had arrived from Poland. Churches were built not only for religious worship, but also as places where Poles could preserve their heritage in a new country. The oldest continuous Polish-Catholic Church in North America was founded by the Kashubs in Wilno, Ontario, in 1876.

Churches, Catholic schools, and housing for the priests were usually clustered together in one area. The Polish Catholics moved to these areas, thus creating a strong Polish community. Owning a home was a primary goal of most Polish immigrants. They saved wisely and invested their savings in homes and neighborhoods.

These early neighborhoods, called *Polonia*, were well organized. They allowed the Poles to keep their traditions alive by speaking Polish, observing traditional customs, and attending Polish-Catholic religious services. Businesses, such as butcher shops, bakeries, grocery stores, and tailoring, were started and flourished in these neighborhoods. Many of the immigrant businesses would allow their customers to buy items on credit and pay for the merchandise at a later date. Almost everyone in these communities spoke Polish, and there was little need to interact with other areas. By building these neighborhoods, the immigrants were establishing their own "Little Polands."

The majority of Americans were not Catholic during the 19th century. Thus, many of the Poles were **shunned** because of their religious beliefs. Other immigrant groups, such as the Irish, Italians, and Germans, were also Catholic. These ethnic groups argued that the Poles should not speak Polish in the Catholic churches and schools. They felt that this was un-American. They wanted the Poles to learn English and blend into their new country.

Education was not a priority for most of the Polish immigrants, particularly the peasants. Their children were considered wage earners for the family, and generally their schooling was minimal. Hard work and the need for material possessions were things that the Poles could understand. Polish parents were anxious to teach their children the qualities of obedience, sharing, and endurance, which they felt would help them as they became adults in America. Thus, it was not uncommon to find Polish children as young as 12 working in the factories. Many children served as **apprentices** to their father or another relative so that they could learn a trade. Education was considered necessary only if a boy wanted to enter the priesthood.

Polish immigrants felt strongly that education was connected to religion and sent their children to Polish-Catholic schools. Most Poles considered sending a child to public schools a poor decision. The parents

The view through the front window of a Polish bakery in Chicago's Polish Village shows an assortment of tasty baked goods.

A group of Polish Americans march in St. Louis during a Veteran's Day parade. Organizations like the Polish National Alliance helped introduce Polish culture and customs into mainstream American life.

trusted the Polish-Catholic schools and believed they would help teach their children values, traditions, and customs from Poland. Most of the teachers at the Polish-Catholic schools were nuns or priests who had been trained in Poland. The children studied subjects such as math, handwriting, grammar, geography, and history just like the public-school children. In addition, they were taught religion and the Polish language. Traits such as discipline, obedience, and family loyalty were also strongly reinforced in the Polish schools.

Even if a Polish child attended school, often he or she also worked to help the family in some way. Girls cleaned houses and assisted in laundry chores for their family or boarders. Boys would work part-time at local businesses. Children also helped feed and take care of chickens, pigs, and cows. Almost every Polish family had a garden, and the children were expected to help with it. Canning fruits and vegetables, making sauerkraut in a barrel, and sewing were all activities that involved children.

The Polish immigrants were a tight-knit group and could be counted on to help their family and friends. Many of the Poles were isolated from other groups of people because of their language and customs. They enjoyed social and recreational gatherings with other Polish immigrants. From these meetings, various organizations and societies were formed. The first Polish society was formed in 1892 in Johnstown, Pennsylvania. Soon, numerous other groups followed. By the 1910s, approximately three-fourths of the Polish immigrant population was a member of at least one society.

Within the Polish communities, the societies served several purposes. They provided benefits for injured workers and helped care for the families of those immigrants who had died in work-related accidents. They also allowed Poles to remember their heritage and share their lives with other Polish immigrants.

The Polish Falcons Alliance was formed in 1893 to promote Polish culture and physical education. Adam Laboda and other men in his community helped organize the Falcons and the Polish National Alliance in Pittsfield, Massachusetts. These groups also assisted newcomers from Poland with financial help and worked to improve living and working conditions for immigrants. The Polish Falcons established **lodges** in communities and elected officers. Serving as an officer was often the first step for many Poles to become involved in political activities in the United States. The Polish Falcons Alliance and the Polish National Alliance are still active organizations today.

The formation of church choirs and Polish choral groups continued the tradition of singing familiar Polish songs. Younger generations of Poles learned traditional music and dances from these groups. The Polish Women's Alliance was organized in 1900, emphasizing education by establishing libraries and cultural programs. Polish women also joined **rosary** societies organized by local Catholic churches. The rosary societies

Pulaski Day is October 11, a day to honor the Polish nobleman Count Casimir Pulaski (1748–1779). Pulaski left Poland after helping with an unsuccessful revolt against Russia. He arrived in Philadelphia in 1777 and enlisted as a volunteer. Congress made him commander of a *cavalry* troop during the Revolutionary War. His troops were named the Pulaski Legion, and he has been called the father of the American cavalry.

Pulaski was mortally wounded in the battle of Savannah. Monuments have been erected in his memory in Savannah and other cities in the United States. President Harry Truman established this official remembrance day in 1946. Parades honoring Casimir Pulaski are held annually, with many Polish Americans marching in traditional costumes. The United States Postal Service has also issued a postage stamp to honor Casimir Pulaski and his achievements.

Casmir Pulaski was a Polish nobleman who immigrated to the United States during the American Revolution. He fought with the Continental Army and was killed at the battle of Savannah in 1779. His memory is honored on October 11, Pulaski Day.

raised money for the churches and offered spiritual support to members.

There were a large number of Polish publications distributed in the Polish neighborhoods. By 1930, approximately 500 Polish publications had been established, but many of these only survived for a short time. These publications maintained the Polish language and informed readers of current events. Community events and activities were among the items printed, establishing an easy way for Poles to maintain contact with one another. Parents used the newspapers and magazines to educate their children about traditions and customs. Articles about Poland or fictional stories set in Poland were included in the newspapers. Most organizations, such as the Polish National Alliance, published newspapers for their members.

Although poor in material wealth, the Polish immigrants were rich

Music has always been an important part of Polish social life. Here, Jozef Pasierb plays a saxophone while marching in a parade with a Polish band.

in their cultural heritage. The Poles brought many distinctive foods to North America, including kielbasa (sausage), stuffed cabbages, pastries, babka (coffeecake), potato pancakes, sauerkraut, and pierogi (filled dumplings). They continued to celebrate Christmas and Easter according to their traditional religious customs. The Poles participated in a Christmas Eve meal called *wigilia* and sang *koledy*—traditional Polish Christmas carols. A large feast was served at Easter with meats, cakes, and brightly colored eggs called *pisanki*. At Easter, the Polish women brought food to the church to be blessed by the priest before serving. The immigrants also created **ornate** scenes made by cutting and folding paper to use as decorations.

Music was an important part of Polish life, and the immigrants brought with them their music and dances to their new country. Immigrant Adam Laboda and his friends enjoyed dancing with other Poles at the company dance hall. Weddings were big events in the Polish culture. Guests would enjoy food, drink, and music for singing and dancing. Dances such as the *krakowiak*, *oberek*, *mazur*, and *polka* were popular at weddings and celebrations. ✺

A Polish-American woman wears traditional clothing as she rides on a float during a parade in Chicago. Interest in Polish culture and history has grown over the past four decades.

6 Current Immigration

Individuals have continued to migrate from Poland to the United States. The numbers are small compared to the great wave that occurred in the 1860–1900 time period. Like Adam Laboda, many of the new immigrants are young men and women hoping to find better jobs and more opportunities in America.

There was an increase in Polish immigrants traveling to North America after World War II. Living conditions in Poland were difficult after the war. Many of these newcomers were admitted to the United States by the Displaced Persons Act of 1948. This act allowed an additional 205,000 *displaced* persons to emigrate in addition to the annual quota. Some of the immigrants were political refugees who had been forced to leave; others wanted to escape the Communist rule in Poland. Although they had more education and skills than the earlier wave of Polish immigrants, their reasons for coming to America were similar. They wanted to improve their lives and raise their families in a free nation. Canada also welcomed many Polish refugees during this time period.

Another wave of immigrants began arriving in the United States in 1980. Many of these people have come to work and earn money, and are not interested in living permanently in the United States. Other immigrants have brought their families and want to make their home in America.

A group of Polish children disembark from the Japanese ship
Fushima Maru, in 1920. The ship has landed in Seattle, Washington.

Americans began to show a renewed interest in ethnic backgrounds
and customs in the early 1970s. Researching family history and tracing
one's roots became popular activities. Although Polish immigrants had
previously been ashamed and embarrassed about their ethnic culture,
people were now expressing interest in Polish history and culture.
There was public demand for ethnic education classes, and member-
ship in ethnic organizations increased. Names were changed to reflect
the correct spelling of Polish surnames, such as the Warren, Michigan,
politician who changed his name from Jacob to Jakubowski. Many

communities established festivals and special events in remembrance of early settlers. A radio station in Sheridan, Wyoming, started a two-hour program called Polka Party to honor the Polish heritage of its residents. The editor of a Polish-American weekly publication in New Jersey started organizing I'm-Proud-to-be-Polish clubs.

According to the 2006 American Community Survey, there are more than 10 million Polish Americans in the United States. This makes them the ninth-largest ancestry group. In Canada, according to the most recent census figures, there are nearly 275,000 people of Polish ancestry. Polish Americans have contributed greatly to the culture and society of the United States and Canada. They remain a vital and vibrant ethnic group of North America.

Isaac Bashevis Singer was born in Poland in 1904 and emigrated to the United States in 1935. Many of his short stories and novels are set in 19th-century Poland. Singer won the Nobel Prize for literature in 1978; he died in 1991.

Chronology

1608 First Polish immigrants arrive in Jamestown; establish first glass factory in America.

1776–1783 Thaddeus Kosciuszko and Casimir Pulaski play important roles in the American Revolutionary War.

1854 The Polish farming community of Panna Maria is founded in Texas.

1858 The Polish immigrant group called Kashubs arrives in Canada.

1870 Steamships begin to replace sailing ships for voyages to North America.

1890 The largest wave of migration begins from Poland to North America.

1892 Ellis Island is established as the official federal immigration station on the east coast; many Polish immigrants are processed there.

1893 The Polish Falcons Alliance is founded.

1897 The Lattimer Massacre occurs in Lattimer, Pennsylvania.

1900 Ninety-five percent of Polish immigrants are employed as industrial workers.

1921 U.S. Congress enacts stricter immigration laws.

1948 The Displaced Persons Refugee Act allows political refugees from Poland to enter the United States.

1980 Political persecution leads to a new wave of Polish immigration to the United States.

2003 Poles rank as the ninth-largest ancestry group in the United States.

2006 The Polish-American population of the United States reaches 10 million.

Immigration Figures

Number of Polish immigration becoming U.S. citizens, by Decade

1820-29:	**19**
1830-39:	**366**
1840-49:	**105**
1850-59:	**1,087**
1860-69:	**1,886**
1870-79:	**11,016**
1880-89:	**42,910**
1890-99:	**107,793**
1900-09:	**——***
1910-19:	**——***
1920-29:	**223,316**
1930-39:	**25,555**
1940-49:	**7,577**
1950-59:	**6,465**
1960-69:	**55,742**
1970-79:	**33,696**
1980-89:	**63,483**
1990-99:	**172,249**
2000-07:	**101,641**

* No data available. From 1894 to 1919, data for Poland was included with Austria-Hungary, Germany, and the Soviet Union.

Source: *Yearbook of Immigration Statistics*, 2007.

Famous Polish Americans

Zbigniew Brzezinski He served as the national security advisor under President Jimmy Carter.

Mike Ditka He played tight end for the Chicago Bears and later coached them to a Super Bowl championship.

Casimir Funk He was a biochemist and the first scientist to discover and use the term "vitamin."

Stanley Haidasz He was the first Polish Liberal Member of the Canadian Parliament. He became minister for multiculturalism in the Pierre Trudeau administration and was the first Polish representative in the Senate.

Ruth Handler She was the co-founder of Mattel toy company and created the Barbie doll.

Jane Krakowski Tony Award-winning actress and singer. She has had major roles on the television shows *Ally McBeal* and *30 Rock*.

Mike Krzyzewski The coach of the Duke University Blue Devils men's basketball team has won three national titles and more than 800 games in his career.

Maria Goeppert Mayer She won the 1963 Nobel Prize in physics for her research on the shell model of the atomic nucleus.

Stan Musial He was a baseball player with the St. Louis Cardinals and won the Most Valuable Player Award three times in his career.

Edmund Muskie He served as governor of Maine and as the U.S. senator from Maine for 21 years. In 1968, he became the first American of Polish background to run for vice-president. His father had changed the family name from Marciszewski.

Tim Pawlenty Elected governor of Minnesota in 2003.

Jim Peplinski He was a Canadian NHL hockey player and was co-captain of the Calgary Flames when they won their first Stanley Cup in 1989.

Arthur Rubinstein He was a concert pianist who was awarded the U.S. Medal of Freedom.

Dr. Albert Sabin He developed the oral polio vaccine.

Maurice Sendak He was an illustrator and author of children's books. His works include *Where The Wild Things Are.*

Isaac Bashevis Singer He was a writer and recipient of the 1978 Nobel Prize for Literature.

Leopold Stokowski He formed the American Symphony Orchestra, conducted the NBC Symphony and Cincinnati Symphony, and organized the All-American Youth Orchestra.

Carl Yastrzemski He was a major league baseball player and played left field for the Boston Red Sox. He was voted to the Baseball Hall of Fame.

Korczak Ziolkowski He was a sculptor and is best known for his work on the Crazy Horse Memorial in South Dakota.

Janusz Zurakowski He was a decorated Polish ace aviator who immigrated to Canada in 1952. He broke the sound barrier in an AVRO CF-100, the first Canadian aircraft to reach that speed, and made the first flight of the AVRO ARROW, an advanced supersonic jet.

Andy and Larry Wachowski Award-winning filmmakers who created the *Matrix* films. Their other movies include *V for Vendetta* and *Speed Racer*.

Glossary

Apprentice a person who learns a skill or trade by working under skilled workers.

Cavalry an army division mounted on horseback.

Deport to send someone out of the country by legal means.

Discrimination an action or treatment based on prejudiced opinions.

Displaced forced to flee from one's home or homeland.

Dormitory a large room containing numerous beds.

Emigrate to leave one's country to live elsewhere.

Executor the person appointed to execute a will.

Export to send goods to another country.

Hearth the section of a furnace on which ore or metal is exposed to heat.

Homestead to acquire or settle on land under a homestead law.

Illiterate unable to read or write.

Immigrant a person who comes to a country to live there permanently.

Lodge the meeting place of a branch of an organization.

Manifest a list of passengers.

Naturalize to grant citizenship to someone of foreign birth.

Ornate elaborately decorated.

Peasant of the lowest, poorest class.

Quota a share of proportion assigned to each member of a group.

Recruit to secure the services of.

Rosary a string of beads used in counting prayers, used primarily in the Roman Catholic faith.

Shun to avoid.

Steerage the cheapest passenger accommodations on board a ship, usually in the area near the rudder and steering gear.

Strike a temporary work stoppage by workers to protest an act or condition.

Further Reading

About the Polish Americans

Bukowczyk, John J. *Polish Americans and Their History*. Pittsburgh: University of Pittsburgh Press, 1996.

Dinnerstein, Leonard and David Reimers. *Ethnic Americans: A History of Immigration*. New York: Columbia University Press, 1999.

Kruszka, Waclaw. *A History of the Poles in America to 1908*. Washington, D.C.: The Catholic University of America Press, 1993.

Marcovitz, Hal. *Ellis Island*. Philadelphia: Mason Crest, 2003.

Pula, James S. *Polish Americans: An Ethnic Community*. New York: Twayne Publishers, 1995.

Finding your Polish American ancestors

Carmack, Sharon DeBartolo. *A Geneaologist's Guide to Discovering Your Immigrant and Ethnic Ancestors*. Cincinnati: Betterway Books, 2000.

Hoffman, William F., and George W. Helon. *First Names of the Polish Commonwealth: Origins and Meanings*. Chicago: Polish Genealogical Society of America, 1998.

Rollyson, Carl Sokolnicki, and Lisa Olson Paddock. *A Student's Guide to Polish American Genealogy*. Phoenix: The Oryx Press, 1996.

Internet Resources

http://www.census.gov

The official Web site of the U.S. Bureau of the Census contains information about the most recent census taken in 2000.

http://www12.statcan.ca/english/census/index.cfm

The Web site for Canada's Bureau of Statistics, which includes population information updated for the most recent census in May 2006.

http://www.hsp.org/

The Web site for the Historical Society of Pennsylvania, dedicated to educating and preserving the state's heritage as a melting pot of diverse peoples.

http://kpk.org/en/

This Web site for the Polish Canadian Research Institute is aimed at representing Polish Canadians in Canada as well as abroad.

http://www.pgsa.org/

This Web site provides information for people seeking to find information on Polish ancestors.

http://www.polishamericancenter.org

This Web site covers practically everything Polish-American: gifts, radio programs, social services, museums and more.

Index

Albany, 12
Alberta, 37
American Immigrant Wall of Honor, 29
Austria, 18

Berkshire Woolen Mill, 15
Bremen, 12
Buffalo, 31

Canada, 29, 36–37, 39, 51, 53
Canadian Pacific Railway, 37
Castle Garden, 24
Chicago, 31
Cleveland, 31
Communist, 51
Connecticut Valley, 35

Detroit, 33
Displaced Persons Act of 1948, 51

Ellis Island, 26, 27, 28, 29
Ellis Island Immigration Museum, 29
English, 15, 24, 42
Europe, 23, 38, 39

Germans, 38
Germany, 11, 12
Gilbertsville, Massachusetts, 12, 13
Great Migration, 17

Irish, 15, 38, 39, 42
Italians, 42

Jamestown, Virginia, 17
Johnstown, Pennsylvania, 47

Kashubs, 37, 41

Kaszuby, 37, 39

Laboda, Adam, 11–15, 21, 35, 38, 45,
    49, 51
Lattimer, Pennsylvania, 32
Lattmier Massacre, 34
Little Poland, 42
Long Island, 35

Manhattan, 24, 29
Manitoba, 37
Massachusetts, 35
Milwaukee, 31
Minnesota, 31, 35
Montreal, 29, 37

New York, 12, 25
New York City, 27, 30
New York Harbor, 12
North Dakota, 31

Ontario, 37, 41

Panna Maria, 17, 31
Pardee Mine, 32
Pennsylvania, 32
Pittsburgh, 30, 31, 33
Pittsfield, Massachusetts, 13, 45
Poland, 11, 13, 17–22, 37, 41, 44, 47,
    51
Polish, 12, 17–18, 25–26, 31, 33–39,
    41–49, 51–53
Polish Falcons Alliance, 45–46
Polish National Alliance, 47
Polish Women's Alliance, 46
Pontoosuc, 15
Prussia, 18

Quebec City, 31

Roman Catholic, 17, 41–44, 46
Russia, 18

Saskatchewan, 37
Scots, 38
South Dakota, 31
Statue of Liberty, 24
Syracuse, 12

Tepper, Regina Sass, 26
Texas, 17, 31
Toronto, 37

United States, 15, 17–18, 24, 29, 31, 33,
    35, 37, 41–44, 47, 51–53
U.S. Congress, 39
U.S. Immigration and Naturalization
    Service, 17

Vancouver, 29

Welsh, 38
Wisconsin, 31, 35
World War II, 51

Zowisezbie, 11, 12

Photo Credits

Contributors

Barry Moreno has been librarian and historian at the Ellis Island Immigration Museum and the Statue of Liberty National Monument since 1988. He is the author of *The Statue of Liberty Encyclopedia*, which was published by Simon & Schuster in October 2000. He is a native of Los Angeles, California. After graduation from California State University at Los Angeles, where he earned a degree in history, he joined the National Park Service as a seasonal park ranger at the Statue of Liberty; he eventually became the monument's librarian. In his spare time, Barry enjoys reading, writing, and studying foreign languages and grammar. His biography has been included in *Who's Who Among Hispanic Americans*, *The Directory of National Park Service Historians*, *Who's Who in America*, and *The Directory of American Scholars*.

Donna Lock is the author of *Sweetheart Town, USA* and co-authored *In The Shadow of Long's Peak*, historical books about Colorado. She has also written business and financial education books. She lives in Fort Collins, Colorado, with her husband and two daughters.